A LITTLE
TREASURY
OF GOLD

FOR MOTHER WITH LOVE

COMPILED BY
KAY ANNE CARSON

INSPIRATIONAL PRESS
NEW YORK

FOR MY VERY SPECIAL MOTHER,
ELSIE MARIE, WITH LOVE

Published in 1994 by
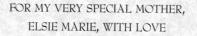
INSPIRATIONAL PRESS
A division of Budget Book Service, Inc.
386 Park Avenue South
Suite 1913
New York, NY 10016

Inspirational Press is a registered trademark
of Budget Book Service, Inc.

Library of Congress Catalog Card Number: 93-80402
ISBN: 0-88486-092-2

Designed by Cindy LaBreacht.
Printed in Hong Kong.

ACKNOWLEDGEMENTS

The compiler and publisher have made every effort to trace the ownership of all copyrighted poems. While expressing regret for any error unintentionally made, the publisher will be pleased to make the necessary correction in future editions of the book.

Sincere thanks are due the following publishers for cooperation in allowing the use of poems selected from their publications:

Alice E. Allen for "My Mother's Garden."

Contemporary Books, Inc. for "Becoming a Dad" from *Collected Verse* by Edgar A. Guest.

Harcourt Brace & Company for "Edgar A. Guest Considers 'The Good Old Woman Who Lived in a Shoe' and the Good Old Truths Simultaneously" from *Selected Poems and Parodies of Louis Untermeyer*, copyright 1935, by Harcourt Brace & Company, Inc.; and "In an Iridescent Time" by Ruth Stone. First published in *The New Yorker* (under the title "Laundry"), copyright © 1958 by Ruth Stone.

Henry Holt and Company, Inc. for "But God's Own Descent" and "The Master Speed" from *The Poetry of Robert Frost* edited by Edward Lathem, copyright © 1975 by Lesley Frost Ballantine, reprinted by permission of Henry Holt and Company, Inc.; and "Nancy Hanks" by Rosemary Carr Benet from *A Book of Americans*, copyright © 1933 by Rosemary and Stephen Vincent Benet.

CONTENTS

MY MOTHER'S GARDEN

Her heart is like her garden,
Old-fashioned, quaint and sweet,
With here a wealth of blossoms,
And there a still retreat.
Sweet violets are hiding,
We know as we pass by,
And lilies, pure as angel thoughts,
Are opening somewhere nigh.

Forget-me-nots there linger,
to full perfection brought,
And there bloom purple pansies
In many a tender thought.
There love's own roses blossom,
As from enchanted ground,
And lavish perfume exquisite
The whole glad year around.

And in that quiet garden—
The garden of her heart—
Songbirds are always singing
Their songs of cheer apart.
And from it floats forever,
O'ercoming sin and strife,
Sweet as the breath of roses blown,
The fragrance of her life.

ALICE E. ALLEN

I.

warm all
the kitchen
with
thy love

THE DIVINE OFFICE OF THE KITCHEN
"God walks among the pots and pipkins"–St. Teresa

Lord of the pots and pipkins, since I have no time to be
A saint by doing lovely things and vigiling with Thee,
By watching in the twilight dawn, and storming Heaven's
      gates,
Make me a saint by getting meals, and washing up the plates!

Lord of the pots and pipkins, please, I offer Thee my souls,
The tiresomeness of tea leaves, and the sticky porridge bowls!
Remind me of the things I need, not just to save the stairs,
But so that I may perfectly lay tables into prayers.

Accept my roughened hands because I made them so for
      Thee!
Pretend my dishmop is a bow, which heavenly harmony
Makes on a fiddle frying pan; it is so hard to clean,
And, ah, so horrid! Hear, dear Lord, the music that I mean!

Although I must have Martha hands, I have a Mary mind,
And when I black the boots, I try Thy sandals, Lord, to find.
I think of how they trod our earth, what time I scrub the
      floor.
Accept this meditation when I haven't time for more!

Vespers and Compline come to pass by washing supper
     things.
And, mostly I am very tired; and all the heart that sings
About the morning's work, is gone, before me into bed.
Lend me, dear Lord, Thy Tireless Heart to work in me
     instead!

My matins are said overnight to praise and bless Thy Name
Beforehand for tomorrow's work, which will be just the same;
So that it seems I go to bed still in my working dress.
Lord make Thy Cinderella soon a heavenly Princess.

Warm all the kitchen with Thy Love and light it with Thy
     Peace!
Forgive the worrying, and make the grumbling words to
     cease.
Lord, who laid Breakfast on the shore, forgive the world
     which saith
"Can any good thing come to God out of poor Nazareth?"

CECILY HALLACK

HUSWIFERY

Make me, O Lord, Thy spinning wheel complete.
Thy Holy Word my distaff make for me.
Make mine affections Thy swift flyers neat
And make my soul Thy holy spool to be.
My conversation make to be Thy reel
And reel the yarn thereon spun of Thy wheel.

Make me Thy loom then, knit therein this twine:
And make Thy Holy Spirit, Lord, wind quills:
Then weave the web Thyself. The yarn is fine.
Thine ordinances make my fulling mills.
Then dye the same in heavenly colors choice,
All pinked with varnished flowers of paradise.

Then clothe therewith mine understanding, will,
Affections, judgment, conscience, memory,
My words, and actions, that their shine may fill
My ways with glory and Thee glorify.
Then mine apparel shall display before Ye
That I am clothed in holy robes for glory.

EDWARD TAYLOR

IN AN IRIDESCENT TIME

My mother, when young, scrubbed laundry in a tub,
She and her sisters on an old brick walk
Under the apple trees, sweet rub-a-dub.
The bees came round their heads, and wrens made talk.
Four young ladies each with a rainbow board
Honed their knuckles, wrung their wrists to red,
Tossed back their braids and wiped their aprons wet.
The Jersey calf beyond the back fence roared;
And all the soft day, swarms about their pet
Buzzed at his big brown eyes and bullish head.
Four times they rinsed, they said. Some things they
    starched,
Then shook them from the baskets two by two,
And pinned the fluttering intimacies of life
Between the lilac bushes and the yew:
Brown gingham, pink, and skirts of Alice blue.

RUTH STONE

EASILY GIVEN

It was only a sunny smile,
    And little it cost in the giving;
        But it scattered the night
        Like morning light,
    And made the day worth living.
Through life's dull warp a woof it wove,
In shining colors of light and love,
And the angels smiled as they watched above,
    Yet little it cost in giving.

It was only a kindly word,
    And a word that was lightly spoken;
        Yet not in vain,
        For it stilled the pain
    Of a heart that was nearly broken.
It strengthened a fate beset by fears
And groping blindly through mists of tears
For light to brighten the coming years,
    Although it was lightly spoken.

It was only a helping hand,
    And it seemed of little availing;
        But its clasps were warm,
        And it saved from harm
    A brother whose strength was failing.
Its touch was tender as angels' wings,
But it rolled the stone from the hidden springs,
And pointed the way to higher things,
    Though it seemed of little availing.

A smile, a word, a touch,
    And each is easily given;
        Yet one may win
        A soul from sin
    Or smooth the way to heaven.
A smile may lighten a falling heart,
A word may soften pain's keenest smart,
A touch may lead us from sin apart—
    How easily each is given!

AUTHOR UNKNOWN

WASHING THE DISHES

When we on simple rations sup
How easy is the washing up!
But heavy feeding complicates
The task by soiling many plates.

And though I grant that I have prayed
That we might find a serving-maid,
I'd scullion all my days, I think,
To see Her smile across the sink!

I wash, she wipes. In water hot
I souse each dish and pan and pot;
While Taffy mutters, purrs, and begs,
And rubs himself against my legs.

The man who never in his life
Has washed the dishes with his wife
Or polished up the silver plate—
He still is largely celibate.

One warning: there is certain ware
That must be handled with all care:
The Lord Himself will give you up
If you should drop a willow cup!

CHRISTOPHER MORLEY

THE READING MOTHER

I had a Mother who read to me
Sagas of pirates who scoured the sea,
Cutlasses clenched in their yellow teeth,
"Blackbirds" stowed in the hold beneath

I had a Mother who read me lays
Of ancient and gallant and golden days;
Stories of Marion and Ivanhoe,
Which every boy has a right to know.

I had a Mother who read me tales
Of Gelert the hound of the hills of Wales,
True to his trust till his tragic death,
Faithfulness blent with his final breath.

I had a Mother who read me the things
That wholesome life to the boy heart brings—
Stories that stir with an upward touch,
Oh, that each mother of boys were such!

You may have tangible wealth untold;
Caskets of jewels and coffers of gold.
Richer than I you can never be—
I had a Mother who read to me.

STRICKLAND GILLILAN

MIS' SMITH

All day she hurried to get through
The same as lots of wimmin do;
Sometimes at night her husban' said,
"Ma, ain't you goin' to come to bed?"
And then she'd kinder give a hitch,
And pause half-way between a stitch,
And sorter sigh, and say that she
  Was ready as she'd ever be,
   She reckoned.

And so the years went one by one,
An' somehow she was never done;
An' when the angel said, as how
"Mis' Smith, it's time you rested now,"
She sorter raised her eyes to look
A second, as a stitch she took;
"All right, I'm comin' now", says she,
  "I'm ready as I'll ever be,
   I reckon."

ALBERT BIGELOW PAINE

I WILL MAKE YOU BROOCHES

I will make you brooches and toys for your delight,
Of bird-song at morning and star-shine at night.
I will build a palace fit for you and me,
Of green days in forests and blue days at sea.

I will make my kitchen, and you shall keep your room,
Where white flows the river and bright blows the broom,
And you shall wash your linen and keep your body white
In rainfall at morning and dewfall at night.

And this shall be for music when no one else is near,
The fine song for singing, the rare song to hear!
That only I remember, that only you admire,
Of the broad road that stretches and the roadside fire.

ROBERT LOUIS STEVENSON

II.

but
the touch
of her
hand

THE WOMAN WHO UNDERSTANDS

Somewhere she waits to make you win, your soul
in her firm, white hands—
Somewhere God has made for you, the Woman
Who Understands!

As the tide went out she found him
Lashed to a spar of Despair,
The wreck of his Ship around him—
The wreck of his Dreams in the air;
Found him and loved him and gathered
The soul of him close to her heart—
The soul that had sailed an uncharted sea,
The soul that had sought to win and be free—
The soul of which she was part!
And there in the dusk she cried to the man,
"Win your battle—you can, you can!"

Broken by Fate, unrelenting,
Scarred by the lashings of Chance;
Bitter his heart—unrepenting—
Hardened by Circumstance;
Shadowed by Failure ever,
Cursing, he would have died,
But the touch of her hand, her strong warm hand,

And her love of his soul, took full command,
　　Just at the turn of the tide!
　　　　Standing beside him, filled with trust,
　　"Win!" she whispered, "you must, you must!"

Helping and loving and guiding,
　　Urging when that were best,
Holding her fears in hiding
　　Deep in her quiet breast;
This is the woman who kept him
　　True to his standards lost,
When tossed in the storm and stress of strife,
He thought himself through with the game of life
　　And ready to pay the cost.
　　　　Watching and guarding, whispering still,
　　　　"Win you can—and you will, you will!"

This is the story of ages
　　This is the Woman's way;
Wiser than seers or sages,
　　Lifting us day by day;
Facing all things with a courage
　　Nothing can daunt or dim,
　　　　Treading Life's path, wherever it leads—

15

Lined with flowers or choked with weeds,
    But ever with him—with him!
        Guidon—comrade—golden spur—
        The men who win are helped by her!

Somewhere she waits, strong in belief, your
    Soul in her firm, white hands:
Thank well your God, when she comes to you,
    The Woman Who Understands!

EVERARD JACK APPLETON

I'LL GIVE MY LOVE AN APPLE

I'll give my love an apple without a core,
I'll give my love a house without a door,
I'll give my love a palace wherein she may be,
And she may unlock it without a key.

My head is the apple without a core,
My mind is the house without a door,
My heart is the palace wherein she may be,
And she may unlock it without any key.

ANONYMOUS

ALL NIGHT THE CICADA CHIRPS

"All night the cicada chirps;
all day the grasshopper jumps.
Before I saw my love,
my heart was confused.
But now that I have seen him,
now that I have met him,
my heart is calm."

"I climbed the southern hill
to pick the fern shoots.
Before I saw my love,
my heart was troubled.
But now that I have seen her,
now that I have met her,
my heart is at peace."

"I climbed the southern hill
to pick the bracken shoots.
Before I saw my love,
my heart was sad.
But now that I have seen her,
now that I have met her,
my heart is serene."

THE BOOK OF SONGS
adapted from the translation of Arthur Waley

IT WAS A QUIET WAY

It was a quiet way—
He asked if I was his—
I made no answer of the Tongue
But answer of the Eyes—
And then He bore me on
Before this mortal noise
With swiftness, as of Chariots
And distance, as of Wheels.
This World did drop away
As Acres from the feet
Of one that leaneth from Balloon
Upon an Ether street.
The Gulf behind was not,
The Continents were new—
Eternity was due.
No Seasons were to us—
It was not Night nor Morn—
But Sunrise stopped upon the place
And fastened it in Dawn.

EMILY DICKINSON

THE MASTER SPEED

No speed of wind or water rushing by
But you have speed far greater. You can climb
Back up a stream of radiance to the sky,
And back through history up the stream of time.
And you were given this swiftness, not for haste
Nor chiefly that you may go where you will,
But in the rush of everything to waste,
That you may have the power of standing still—
Off any still or moving thing you say.
Two such as you with such a master speed
Cannot be parted nor be swept away
From one another once you are agreed
That life is only life forevermore
Together wing to wing and oar to oar.

ROBERT FROST

THE OWL AND THE PUSSY-CAT

The Owl and the Pussy-Cat went to sea
  In a beautiful pea-green boat:
They took some honey, and plenty of money
  Wrapped up in a five-pound note.
The Owl looked up to the stars above,
  And sang to a small guitar,
"O lovely Pussy, O Pussy, my love,
  What a beautiful Pussy you are,
    You are,
    You are!
  What a beautiful Pussy you are!"

Pussy said to the Owl, "You elegant fowl,
  How charmingly sweet you sing!
Oh! let us be married; too long we have tarried:
  But what shall we do for a ring?"
They sailed away, for a year and a day,
  To the land where the bong-tree grows;
And there in a wood a Piggy-wig stood,
  With a ring at the end of his nose,
    His nose,
    His nose,
  With a ring at the end of his nose.

"Dear Pig, are you willing to sell for one shilling
    Your ring?" Said the Piggy, "I will."
So they took it away, and were married next day
    By the Turkey who lives on the hill.
They dined on mince and slices of quince,
    Which they ate with a runcible spoon;
And hand in hand, on the edge of the sand,
    They danced by the light of the moon,
        The moon,
        The moon,
    They danced by the light of the moon.

EDWARD LEAR

HOME

O, Falmouth is a fine town with ships in the bay,
And I wish from my heart it's there I was to-day;
I wish from my heart I was far away from here,
Sitting in my parlor and talking to my dear.
For it's home, dearie, home—it's home I want to be.
Our topsails are hoisted, and we'll away to sea.
O, the oak and the ash and the bonnie birken tree
They're all growing green in the old countrie.

In Baltimore a-walking a lady I did meet
With her babe on her arm as she came down the street;
And I thought how I sailed, and the cradle standing ready
For the pretty little babe that had never seen its daddie.
    And it's home, dearie, home,—

O, if it be a lass, she shall wear a golden ring;
And if it be a lad, he shall fight for his king;
With his dirk and his hat and his little jacket blue
He shall walk the quarter-deck as his daddie used to do.
    And it's home, dearie, home,—

O, there's a wind a-blowing, a-blowing from the west,
And that of all the winds is the one I like the best,
For it blows at our backs, and it shakes our pennon free,
And it soon will blow us home to the old countrie.
For it's home, dearie, home—it's home I want to be.
Our topsails are hoisted, and we'll away to sea.
O, the oak and the ash and the bonnie birken tree
They're all growing green in the old countrie.

WILLIAM ERNEST HENLEY

FOR HER SAKE

Her world is all aware. She reads
omens in small happenings, the fall of a teaspoon,
flurries of birds, a cat's back arching,
words unspoken, wine spilt.
She will notice moods in handwriting,
be tuned to feelings in a room,
sense ill-luck in a house, take heed of ghosts,
hear children cry before the sound has reached her,
stay unperturbed in storms, keep silence
where speech would spoil. Days are her changes,
weather her time.

Whether it be becalmed in cool mornings
of air and water, or thunderstruck through nights
where flesh craves and is answered, in her, love
knows no division, is an incarnation
all of her wonder, as she makes
madness subside, and all thought-splintered things
grow whole again.

Look below. She walks in the garden,
preoccupied with paths, head bent,
beautiful, not at rest, as objects are,
but moving, in the fleck of light and shade.

24

Her ways are hers, not mine. Pointless to make
my sense of her, or claim her faithfulness.
She is as women are, aware
of her own mystery, in her way faithful
to flowers and days; and from the window's distance,
I watch her, haunted by her otherness.

Well to love true women, whose whims are wise,
whose world is warm, whose home is time,
and well to pleasure them, since, last of all,
they are the truth which men must tell,
and in their pleasure, houses lighten,
gardens grow fruitful, and true tales are told.
Well to move from mind's distance
into their aura, where the air
is shifting, intimate, particular.

And of true women, she, whose eyes illumine
this day I wake in—well to mark
her weather, how her look is candid,
her voice clear-toned, her heart private,
her love both wild and reticent.
Well to praise and please her, well to make
this for her sake.

ALASTAIR REID

MY HEART IS LIKE A SINGING BIRD

My heart is like a singing bird
    Whose nest is in a watered shoot:
My heart is like an apple-tree
    Whose boughs are bent with thickset fruit;
My heart is like a rainbow shell
    That paddles in a halcyon sea;
My heart is gladder than all these
    Because my love is come to me.

Raise me a dais of silk and down;
    Hang it with vair and purple dyes;
Carve it in doves and pomegranates,
    And peacocks with a hundred eyes;
Work it in gold and silver grapes,
    In leaves and silver fleurs-de-lys;
Because the birthday of my life
    Is come, my love is come to me.

CHRISTINA ROSSETTI

I GAVE MYSELF TO HIM

I gave myself to Him—
And took Himself, for Pay,
The solemn contract of a Life
Was ratified, this way—

The Wealth might disappoint
Myself a poorer prove
Than this great Purchaser suspect,
The Daily Own—of Love

Depreciate the Vision—
But till the Merchant buy—
Still Fable—in the Isles of Spice—
The subtle Cargoes—lie—

At least—'tis Mutual—Risk—
Some—found it—Mutual Gain—
Sweet Debt of Life—Each Night to owe—
Insolvent—every Noon—

EMILY DICKINSON

THERE IS NOTHING FALSE IN THEE

There is nothing false in thee.
In thy heat the youngest body
Has warmth and light.
In thee the quills of the sun
Find adornment.
What does not die
Is with thee.

Thou art clothed in robes of music.
Thy voice awakens wings.

And still more with thee
Are the flowers of earth made bright.

Upon thy deeps the fiery sails
Of heaven glide.

Thou art the radiance and the joy.
Thy heart shall only fail
When all else has fallen.

What does not perish
Lives in thee.

KENNETH PATCHEN

THAT TIME OF YEAR
THOU MAYST IN ME BEHOLD

That time of year thou mayst in me behold
When yellow leaves, or none, or few, do hang
Upon those boughs which shake against the cold,
Bare ruin'd choirs where late the sweet birds sang.
In me thou see'st the twilight of such day
As after sunset fadeth in the west,
Why by and by black night doth take away,
Death's second self, that seals up all in rest.
In me thou see'st the glowing of such fire,
That on the ashes of his youth doth lie,
As the death-bed whereon it must expire,
Consum'd with that which it was nourish'd by.
    This thou perceiv'st, which makes thy love more strong,
    To love that well which thou must leave ere long.

WILLIAM SHAKESPEARE

POEM IN PROSE

This poem is for my wife
I have made it plainly and honestly
The mark is on it
Like the burl on the knife

I have not made it for praise
She has no more need for praise
Than summer has
On the bright days

In all that becomes a woman
Her words and her ways are beautiful
Love's lovely duty
The well-swept room

Wherever she is there is sun
And time and a sweet air
Peace is there
Work done

There are always curtains and flowers
And candles and baked bread
And a cloth spread
And a clean house

Her voice when she sings is a voice
At dawn by a freshening sea
Where the wave leaps in the
Wind and rejoices

Wherever she is it is now
It is here where the apples are
Here in the stars
In the quick hour

The greatest and richest good—
My own life to live—
This she has given me

If giver could

ARCHIBALD MAC LEISH

BEFORE THE BIRTH OF ONE
OF HER CHILDREN

All things within this fading world hath end,
Adversity doth still our joys attend;
No ties so strong, no friends so dear and sweet,
But with death's parting blow is sure to meet.
The sentence past is most irrevocable,
A common thing, yet oh, inevitable.
How soon, my Dear, death may my steps attend,
How soon't may be thy lot to lose thy friend,
We both are ignorant, yet love bids me
These farewell lines to recommend to thee,
That when that knot's untied that made us one,
I may seem thine, who in effect am none.
And if I see not half my days that's due,
What nature would, God grant to yours and you;
The many faults that well you know I have
Let be interred in my oblivious grave;

If any worth or virtue were in me,
Let that live freshly in thy memory
And when thou feel'st no grief, as I no harms,
Yet love thy dead, who long lay in thine arms.
And when thy loss shall be repaid with gains
Look to my little babes, my dear remains.
And if thou love thyself, or loved'st me,
These O protect from step-dame's injury.
And if chance to thine eyes shall bring this verse,
With some sad sighs honour my absent hearse;
And kiss this paper for thy love's dear sake,
Who with salt tears this last farewell did take.

ANNE BRADSTREET

III.

above me
the patter
of little
feet

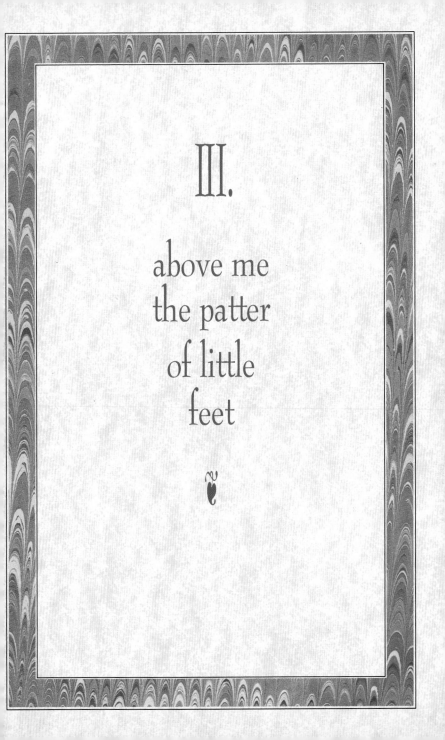

THE CHILDREN'S HOUR

Between the dark and the daylight,
    When the night is beginning to lower,
Comes a pause in the day's occupations,
    That is known as the Children's Hour.

I hear in the chamber above me
    The patter of little feet,
The sound of a door that is opened,
    And voices soft and sweet.

From my study I see in the lamplight,
    Descending the broad hall stair,
Grave Alice, and laughing Allegra,
    And Edith with golden hair.

A whisper, and then a silence:
    Yet I know by their merry eyes
They are plotting and planning together
    To take me by surprise.

A sudden rush from the stairway,
    A sudden raid from the hall!
By three doors left unguarded
    They enter my castle wall!

They climb up into my turret
      O'er the arms and back of my chair;
If I try to escape, they surround me;
      They seem to be everywhere.

They almost devour me with kisses,
      Their arms about me entwine
Till I think of the Bishop of Bingen
      In his Mouse-Tower on the Rhine!

Do you think, O blue-eyed banditti,
      Because you have scaled the wall,
Such an old mustache as I am
      Is not a match for you all!

I have you fast in my fortress,
      And I will not let you depart,
But put you down into the dungeon
      In the round-tower of my heart.

And there will I keep you forever,
      Yes, forever and a day,
Till the walls shall crumble to ruin,
      And moulder in dust away.

HENRY WADSWORTH LONGFELLOW

SWEET AND LOW

Sweet and low, sweet and low,
    Wind of the western sea,
Low, low, breathe and blow,
    Wind of the western sea!
Over the rolling waters go,
Come from the dying moon, and blow,
    Blow him again to me;
While my little one, while my pretty one sleeps.

Sleep and rest, sleep and rest,
    Father will come to thee soon;
Rest, rest, on mother's breast,
    Father will come to thee soon;
Father will come to his babe in the nest,
Silver sails all out of the west
    Under the silver moon;
Sleep, my little one, sleep, my pretty one, sleep.

ALFRED, LORD TENNYSON

CRADLE SONG

Sleep, sleep, beauty bright,
Dreaming in the joys of night;
Sleep, sleep; in thy sleep
Little sorrows sit and weep.

Sweet babe, in thy face
Soft desires I can trace,
Secret joys and secret smiles,
Little pretty infant wiles.

As thy softest limbs I feel
Smiles as of the morning steal
O'er thy cheek, and o'er thy breast
Where thy little heart doth rest.

O the cunning wiles that creep
In thy little heart asleep!
When thy little heart doth wake,
Then the dreadful night shall break.

WILLIAM BLAKE

I REMEMBER, I REMEMBER

I remember, I remember,
The house where I was born,
The little window where the sun
Came peeping in at morn;
He never came a wink too soon,
Nor brought too long a day,
But now, I often wish the night
Had borne my breath away!

I remember, I remember,
The roses, red and white,
The violets, and the lily-cups,
Those flowers made of light!
The lilacs where the robin built,
And where my brother set
The laburnum on his birthday,–
The tree is living yet!

THOMAS HOOD

UPON HER SOOTHING BREAST

Upon her soothing breast
She lulled her little child;
A winter sunset in the west,
A dreary glory smiled.

EMILY BRONTE

A CHILD'S GRACE

Here a little child I stand
Heaving up my either hand;
Cold as paddocks though they be,
Here I lift them up to Thee,
For a benison to fall
On our meat and on us all. Amen.

ROBERT HERRICK

THE BLUE BOWL

REWARD

All day I did the little things,
The little things that do not show;
I brought the kindling for the fire
I set the candles in a row,
I filled a bowl with marigolds,
The shallow bowl you love the best—
And made the house a pleasant place
Where weariness might take its rest.

The hours sped on, my eager feet
Could not keep pace with my desire.
So much to do, so little time!
I could not let my body tire;
Yet, when the coming of the night
Blotted the garden from my sight,
And on the narrow, graveled walks
Between the guarding flower stalks
I heard your step; I was not through
With services I meant for you.

You came into the quiet room
That glowed enchanted with the bloom
Of yellow flame. I saw your face,
Illumined by the firelit space,
Slowly grow still and comforted—
"It's good to be at home," you said.

BLANCHE BANE KUDER

A WONDERFUL MOTHER

God made a wonderful mother,
A mother who never grows old;
He made her smile of the sunshine,
And He molded her heart of pure gold;
In her eyes He placed bright shining stars,
On her cheeks, fair roses you see;
God made a wonderful mother,
And He gave that dear mother to me.

PAT O'REILLY

EDGAR A. GUEST CONSIDERS
"THE GOOD OLD WOMAN WHO LIVED
IN A SHOE" AND THE GOOD OLD TRUTHS
SIMULTANEOUSLY

It takes a heap o' children to make a home that's true,
And home can be a palace grand or just a plain, old
    shoe;
But if it has a mother dear and a good old dad or two,
Why that's the sort of good old home for good old me
    and you.
Of all the institutions this side the Vale of Rest
Howe'er it be it seems to me a good old mother's best;
And fathers are a blessing, too, they give the place a
    tone;
In fact each child should try to have some parents
    of his own.
The food can be quite simple; just a sop of milk and
    bread
Are plenty when the kiddies know it's time to go to
    bed.

And every little sleepy-head will dream about the day
When he can go to work because a Man's Work is his
    Play.
And, oh, how sweet his life will seem, with nought to
    make him cross,
And he will never watch the clock and always mind
    the boss.
And when he thinks (as may occur), this thought will
    please him best:
That ninety million think the same—including
                 Eddie Guest.

LOUIS UNTERMEYER

A CRADLE SONG

The angels are stooping
Above your bed;
They weary of trooping
With the whimpering dead.

God's laughing in heaven
To see you so good;
The Shining Seven
Are gay with his mood.

I kiss you and kiss you,
My pigeon, my own;
Ah, how I shall miss you
When you have grown.

WILLIAM BUTLER YEATS

SOCIAL STUDIES

Woody says, "Let's *make* our soap,
It's easy.
We learned about it
In school."
He told Mother,
"All you do is
Take a barrel.
Bore holes in the sides,
And fill it with straw.
Ashes on top–"

"No," said Mother.

MARY NEVILLE

A PRAYER FOR MY DAUGHTER

Once more the storm is howling, and half hid
Under this cradle-hood and coverlid
My child sleeps on. There is no obstacle
But Gregory's wood and one bare hill
Whereby the haystack and roof levelling wind,
Bred on the Atlantic, can be stayed;
And for an hour I have walked and prayed
Because of the great gloom that is in my mind.

I have walked and prayed for this young child an hour
And heard the sea-wind scream upon the tower,
And under the arches of the bridge, and scream
In the elms above the flooded stream;
Imagining in excited reverie
That in the future years had come,
Dancing to a frenzied drum,
Out of the murderous innocence of the sea.

May she be granted beauty and yet not
Beauty to make a stranger's eye distraught,
Or hers before a looking-glass, for such,
Being made beautiful overmuch,
Consider beauty a sufficient end,
Lose natural kindness and maybe
The heart—revealing intimacy
That chooses right, and never finds a friend.

Helen being chosen found life flat and dull
And later had much trouble from a fool,
While that great Queen, that rose out of the spray,
Being fatherless could have her way,
Yet chose a bandy-legged smith for man.
It's certain that fine women eat
A crazy salad with their meat,
Whereby the Horn of Plenty is undone.

In courtesy I'd have her chiefly learned,
Hearts are not had as a gift, but hearts are earned
By those that are not entirely beautiful;
Yet many, that have played the fool
For beauty's very self, has charm made wise,
And many a poor man that has roved,
Loved and thought himself beloved,
From a glad kindness cannot take his eyes.

May she become a flourishing hidden tree
That all her thoughts may like the linnet be
And have no business but dispensing round
Their magnanimities of sound,
Nor but in merriment begin a chase,
Not but in merriment a quarrel.
Oh, may she live like some green laurel
Rooted in one dear perpetual place.

My mind, because the minds that I have loved,
The sort of beauty that I have approved,
Prosper but little, has dried up of late,
Yet knows that to be choked with hate
May well be of all evil chances chief.
If there's no hatred in a mind
Assault and battery of the wind
Can never tear the linnet from the leaf.

An intellectual hatred is the worst,
So let her think opinions are accursed.
Have I not seen the loveliest woman born
Out of the mouth of Plenty's horn,
Because of her opinionated mind
Barter that horn and every good
By quiet natures understood
For an old bellows full of angry wind?

Considering that, all hatred driven hence,
The soul recovers radical innocence
And learns at last that it is self-delighting,
Self-appeasing, self-affrighting,
And that its own sweet will is heaven's will;
She can, though every face should scowl
And every windy quarter howl
Or every bellows burst, be happy still.

And may her bridegroom bring her to a house
Where all's accustomed, ceremonious;
For arrogance and hatred are the wares
Peddled in the thoroughfares.
How but in custom and in ceremony
Are innocence and beauty born?
Ceremony's a name for the rich horn,
And custom for the spreading laurel tree.

WILLIAM BUTLER YEATS

A PARENTAL ODE TO MY SON
Aged Three Years and Five Months

Thou happy, happy elf!
(But stop,–first let me kiss away that tear!)
Thou tiny image of myself!
(My love, he's poking peas into his ear!)
Thou merry, laughing sprite,
With spirits feather-light,
Untouched by sorrow, and unsoiled by sin,–
(My dear, the child is swallowing a pin!)

Thou little tricksy Puck!
With antic toys so funnily bestuck,
Light as the singing bird that wings the air,–
(The door! the door! he'll tumble down the stair!)
Thou darling of thy sire!
(Why, Jane, he'll set his pinafore afire!)
Thou imp of mirth and joy!
In Love's dear chain so strong and a bright a link,
Thou idol of thy parents,–(Drat the boy!
There goes my ink!)

Thou cherub,–but of earth;
Fit playfellow for Fays, by moonlight pale,
In harmless sport and mirth,

(That dog will bite him, if he pulls its tail!)
    Thou human humming-bee, extracting honey
From every blossom in the world that blows,
    Singing in youth's Elysium ever sunny.–
(Another tumble! That's his precious nose!)

Thy father's pride and hope!
(He'll break the mirror with that skipping-rope!)
With pure heart newly stamped from nature's mint,
(Where did he learn that squint?)
Thou young domestic dove!
(He'll have that jug off with another shove!)
Dear nursling of the hymeneal nest!
(Are these torn clothes his best?)
Little epitome of man!
(He'll climb upon the table, that's his plan!)
Touched with the beauteous tints of dawning life,–
    (He's got a knife!)

Thou enviable being!
No storms, no clouds, in thy blue sky foreseeing,
    Play on, play on,
    My elfin John!

Toss the light ball, bestride the stick,—
(I knew so many cakes would make him sick!)
    With fancies, buoyant as the thistle-down,
Prompting the face grotesque, and antic brisk,
With many a lamb-like frisk!
    (He's got the scissors, snipping at your gown!)

Thou pretty opening rose!
(Go to your mother, child, and wipe your nose!)
Balmy and breathing music like the South,—
(He really brings my heart into my mouth!)
Fresh as the morn, and brilliant as its star,—
(I wish that window had an iron bar!)
Bold as the hawk, yet gentle as the dove;—
(I'll tell you what, my love,
I cannot write unless he's sent above.)

THOMAS HOOD

APOLOGY FOR YOUTH

Stand at my window;
watch them pass;
a lass and a lad,
a lad and a lass.

This is a way
to go to school,
learning an olden,
golden rule.

They seek for wisdom
in a book;
then they look up
and look—and look.

And wonder, wonder
if, after all,
wisdom is so
reciprocal.

They ask for beauty,
ask for truth
who have no thought
to ask for youth.

Theirs are the earth,
the sea, the sky;
they sing; they dance,
they float; they fly.

Why do they hurry,
hurry so?
Can they or will they
or do they know

They will earn some love;
they will learn some truth,
but never learn
nor earn back youth.

Stand at my window,
lad and lass;
let not this youth,
this young love pass.

Hold the wonder;
love the lore
you would one day change
the slow years for.

SISTER M. MADELEVA, C.S.C.

MY EARLY HOME

Here sparrows build upon the trees,
    And stock-dove hides her nest;
The leaves are winnowed by the breeze
    Into a calmer rest:
The blackcap's song was very sweet,
    That used the rose to kiss;
It made the paradise complete:
    My early home was this.

The redbreast from the sweetbrier bush
    Dropt down to pick the worm;
On the horse-chestnut sang the thrush,
    O'er the house where I was born;
The moonlight, like a shower of pearls,
    Fell o'er this "bower of bliss,"
And on the bench sat boys and girls:
    My early home was this.

The old house stooped just like a cave,
    Thatched o'er with mosses green;
Winter around the walls would rave,
    But all was calm within;
The trees are here all green agen,
    Here bees and flowers still kiss,
But flowers and trees seemed sweeter then:
    My early home was this.

JOHN CLARE

NANCY HANKS

If Nancy Hanks
Came back as a ghost,
Seeking news
Of what she loved most,
She'd ask first,
"Where's my son?
What's happened to Abe?
What's he done?
"Poor little Abe,
Left all alone
Except for Tom,
Who's a rolling stone;
He was only nine
The year I died.
I remember still
How hard he cried.

"Scraping along
In a little shack
With hardly a shirt
To cover his back,
And a prairie wind
To blow him down,
Or pinching times
If he went to town.

"You wouldn't know
About my son?
Did he grow tall?
Did he have fun?
Did he learn to read?
Did he get to town?
Do you know his name?
Did he get on?"

ROSEMARY BENET

BECOMING A DAD

Old women say that men don't know
The pain through which all mothers go,
And maybe that is true, and yet
I vow I never shall forget
The night he came. I suffered, too,
Those bleak and dreary long hours through;
I paced the floor and mopped my brow
And waited for his glad wee-ow!
I went upstairs and then came down,
Because I saw the doctor frown
And knew beyond the slightest doubt
He wished to goodness I'd clear out.

I walked into the yard for air
And back again to hear her there,
And met the nurse, as calm as though
My world was not in deepest woe,
And when I questioned, seeking speech
Of consolation that would reach
Into my soul and strengthen me
For dreary hours that were to be:
"Progressing nicely!" that was all
She said and tip-toed down the hall;
"Progressing nicely!" nothing more,
And left me there to pace the floor.

And once the nurse came out in haste
For something that had been misplaced,
And I that had been growing bold
Then felt my blood grow icy cold;
And fear's stern chill swept over me.
I stood and watched and tried to see
Just what it was she came to get.
I haven't learned that secret yet.
I half-believe that nurse in white
Was adding fuel to my fright
And taking an unholy glee,
From time to time, in torturing me.

Then silence! To her room I crept
And was informed the doctor slept!
The doctor slept! Oh, vicious thought,
While she at death's door bravely fought
And suffered untold anguish deep,
The doctor lulled himself to sleep.
I looked and saw him stretched out flat
And could have killed the man for that.
Then morning broke, and oh, the joy:
With dawn there came to us our boy.
And in a glorious little while
I went in there and saw her smile!

I must have looked a human wreck,
My collar wilted at my neck,
My hair awry, my features drawn
With all the suffering I had borne.
She looked at me and softly said,
"If I were you, I'd go to bed."
Her's was the bitterer part, I know;
She traveled through the vale of woe.
But now when women folks recall
The pain and anguish of it all
I answer them in manner sad:
"It's no cinch to become a dad."

EDGAR A. GUEST

ON MY FIRST SON

Farewell, thou child of my right hand, and joy;
    My sin was too much hope of thee, loved boy.
Seven years thou wert lent to me, and I thee pay,
    Exacted by thy fate, on the just day.
Oh, could I lose all father now! For why
    Will man lament the state he should envy?
To have so soon 'scaped world's and flesh's rage,
    And, if no other misery, yet age?
Rest in soft peace, and, asked, say here doth lie
    Ben Jonson his best piece of poetry;
For whose sake, henceforth, all his vows be such,
    As what he loves may never like too much.

BEN JONSON

MUTTERINGS OVER THE CRIB
OF A DEAF CHILD

"How will he hear the bell at school
Arrange the broken afternoon,
And know to run across the cool
Grasses where the starlings cry,
Or understand the day is gone?"

Well, someone lifting curious brows
Will take the measure of the clock.
And he will see the birchen boughs
Outside sagging dark from the sky,
And the shade crawling upon the rock.

"And how will he know to rise at morning?
His mother has other sons to waken,
She has the stove she must build to burning
Before the coals of the nighttime die;
And he never stirs when he is shaken."

I take it the air affects the skin,
And you remember, when you were young,
Sometimes you could feel the dawn begin,
And the fire would call you, by and by,
Out of bed and bring you along.

"Well, good enough. To serve his needs
All kinds of arrangements can be made.
But what you will do if his finger bleeds?
Or a bobwhite whistles invisibly
And flutes like an angel off in the shade?"

He will learn pain. And, as for the bird,
It is always darkening when that comes out.
I will putter as though I had not heard,
And lift him into my arms and sing
Whether he hears my song or not.

JAMES WRIGHT

IN MEMORY OF MY DEAR GRANDCHILD
ANNE BRADSTREET
WHO DECEASED JUNE 20, 1669
BEING THREE YEARS AND SEVEN MONTHS OLD

With troubled heart and trembling hand I write,
The heavens have changed to sorrow my delight,
How oft with disappointment have I met,
When I on fading things my hopes have set?
Experience might 'fore this have made me wise,
To value things according to their price.
Was ever stable joy yet found below?
Or perfect bliss without mixture of woe?
I knew she was but as a withering flower,
That's here today, perhaps gone in an hour;
Like as a bubble, or the brittle glass,
Or like a shadow turning as it was.
More fool then I look to look on that was lent
As if mine own, when thus impermanent.
Farewell dear child, thou ne'er shall come to me,
But yet a while, and I shall go to thee;
Mean time my throbbing heart's cheered up with this:
Thou with thy Saviour art in endless bliss.

ANNE BRADSTREET

TO MY SON

I will not say to you, "This is the way; walk in it."
For I do not know your way or where the Spirit may call
        you.
It may be to paths I have never trod or ships on the sea
        leading to unimagined lands afar,
Or haply, to a star!
Or yet again
Through dark and perilous places racked with pain and full
        of fear
Your road may lead you far away from me or near—
I cannot guess or guide, but only stand aside.
Just this I say:
I know for every truth there is a way for each to walk, a
        right for each to choose, a truth to use.
And though you wander far, your soul will know that true
        path when you find it.
Therefore, go!
I will fear nothing for you day or night!
I will not grieve at all because your light is called by some
        new name;
Truth is the same!
It matters nothing to call it star or sun—
All light is one.

AUTHOR UNKNOWN

CHILD'S EVENING HYMN

Now the day is over,
    Night is drawing nigh,
Shadows of the evening
    Steal across the sky.

Now the darkness gathers,
    Stars begin to peep,
Birds and beasts and flowers
    Soon will be asleep.

Jesus give the weary
    Calm and sweet repose,
With thy tenderest blessing
    May our eyelids close.

Grant to little children
    Visions bright of thee,
Guard the sailors tossing
    On the deep blue sea.

Comfort every sufferer
    Watching late in pain;
Those who plan some evil
    From their sin restrain.

Through the long night-watches
    May thy angels spread
Their white wings above me,
    Watching round my bed.

When the morning wakens,
    Then may I arise
Pure and fresh and sinless
    In thy holy eyes.

SABINE BARING-GOULD

NOBODY KNOWS BUT MOTHER

How many buttons are missing today?
    Nobody knows but Mother.
How many playthings are strewn in her way?
    Nobody knows but Mother.
How many thimbles and spools has she missed?
How many burns on each fat little fist?
How many bumps to be cuddled and kissed?
    Nobody knows but Mother.

How many hats has she hunted today?
    Nobody knows but Mother.
Carelessly hiding themselves in the hay–
    Nobody knows but Mother.
How many handkerchiefs wilfully strayed?
How many ribbons for each little maid?
How for her care can a mother be paid?
    Nobody knows but Mother.

How many muddy shoes all in a row?
    Nobody knows but Mother.
How many stockings to darn, do you know?
    Nobody knows but Mother.

How many little torn aprons to mend?
How many hours of toil must she spend?
What is the time when her day's work shall end?
    Nobody knows but Mother.

How many lunches for Tommy and Sam?
    Nobody knows but Mother.
Cookies and apples and blackberrry jam—
    Nobody knows but Mother.
Nourishing dainties for every "sweet tooth,"
Toddling Dottie or dignified Ruth—
How much love sweetens the labor, forsooth?
    Nobody knows but Mother.

How many cares does a mother's heart know?
    Nobody knows but Mother.
How many joys from her mother love flow?
    Nobody knows but Mother.
How many prayers for each little white bed?
How many tears for her babes has she shed?
How many kisses for each curly head?
    Nobody knows but Mother.

MARY MORRISON

IV.

supreme
merit
lay in

risking
spirit

BUT GOD'S OWN DESCENT

But God's own descent
Into flesh was meant
As a demonstration
That the supreme merit
Lay in risking spirit
In substantiation.

Spirit enters flesh
And for all it's worth
Charges into earth
In birth after birth
Ever fresh and fresh.
We may take the view
That its derring-do
Thought of in the large
Is one mighty charge
On our human part
Of the soul's ethereal
Into the material.

ROBERT FROST
from "Kitty Hawk"

74

THE OAK

Live thy Life,
    Young and old,
Like yon oak,
Bright in spring,
    Living gold;

Summer-rich
    Then; and then
Autumn-changed,
Soberer-hued
    Gold again.

All his leaves
    Fallen at length,
Look, he stands,
Trunk and bough,
    Naked strength.

ALFRED, LORD TENNYSON

BY DOING GOOD WE LIVE

A CERTAIN wise man, deeply versed
    In all the learning of the East,
Grew tired in spirit, and athirst
    From life to be released.

So to Eliab, holy man
    Of God he came: "Ah, give me, friend,
The herb of death, that now the span
    Of my vain life may end."

Eliab gently answered: "Ere
    The soul may free itself indeed,
This herb of healing thou must bear
    To seven men in need;

"When thou hast lightened each man's grief,
    And brought him hope and joy again,
Return; nor shalt though seek relief
    At Allah's hands in vain."

The wise man sighed, and humbly said:
    "As Allah willeth, so is best."
And with the healing herb he sped
    Away upon his quest.

And as he journeyed on, intent
    To serve the sorrowing in the land
On deeds of love and mercy bent,
    The herb bloomed in his hand,

And through his pulses shot a fire
    Of strength and hope and happiness;
His heart leaped with a glad desire
    To live and serve and bless.

Lord of all earthly woe and need,
    Be this, life's flower, mine!
To love, to comfort, and to heal–
    Therein is life divine!

JOSEPHINE TROUP

SPEAK OUT

If you have a friend worth loving,
    Love him. Yes, and let him know
That you love him, ere life's evening
    Tinge his brow with sunset glow.
Why should good words ne'er be said
Of a friend—till he is dead?

If you hear a song that thrills you,
    Sung by any child of song,
Praise it. Do not let the singer
    Wait deserved praises long.
Why should one who thrills your heart
Lack the joy you may impart?

If you hear a prayer that moves you
    By its humble, pleading tone,
Join it. Do not let the seeker
    Bow before his God alone.
Why should not thy brother share
The strength of "two or three" in prayer?

If your work is made more easy
    By a friendly, helping hand,
Say so. Speak out brave and truly,
    Ere the darkness veil the land.
Should a brother workman dear
Falter for a word of cheer?

Scatter thus your seeds of kindness
    All enriching as you go—
Leave them. Trust the Harvest-Giver;
    He will make each seed to grow.
So, until the happy end,
Your life shall never lack a friend.

AUTHOR UNKNOWN

THE HOUSE BY THE SIDE OF THE ROAD

THERE ARE hermit souls that live withdrawn
　　In the peace of their self-content;
There are souls, like stars, that dwell apart
　　In a fellowless firmament;
There are pioneer souls that blaze their paths
　　Where highways never ran—
But let me live by the side of the road
　　And be a friend to man.

Let me live in a house by the side of the road,
　　Where the race of men go by—
The men who are good and the men who are bad,
　　As good and as bad as I.
I would not sit in the scorner's seat,
　　Or hurl the cynic's ban—
Let me live in a house by the side of the road,
　　And be a friend to man.

I see from my house by the side of the road,
　　By the side of the highway of life,
The men who press with the ardor of hope
　　The men who are faint with the strife.
But I turn not away from their smiles nor their tears—

Both parts of an infinite plan—
Let me live in a house by the side of the road
And be a friend to man.

I know there are brook-gladdened meadows ahead
And mountains of wearisome height;
And the road passes on through the long afternoon
And stretches away to the night.
But still I rejoice when the travelers rejoice,
And weep with the strangers that moan,
Nor live in my house by the side of the road
Like a man who dwells alone.

Let me live in my house by the side of the road
Where the race of men go by—
They are good, they are bad, they are weak, they are
strong,
Wise, foolish—so am I.
Then why should I sit in the scorner's seat
Or hurl the cynic's ban?
Let me live in my house by the side of the road
And be a friend to man.

SAM WALTER FOSS

HEART'S CONTENT

"A sail! a sail! Oh, whence away,
  And whither, o'er the foam?
Good brother mariners, we pray,
  God speed you safely home!"
"Now wish us not so foul a wind,
  Until the fair be spent;
For hearth and home we leave behind:
  We sail for Heart's Content."

"For Heart's Content! And sail ye so,
  With canvas flowing free?
But, pray you, tell us, if ye know,
  Where may that harbor be?
For we that greet you, worn of time,
  Wave-racked, and tempest-rent,
By sun and star, in every clime,
  Have searched for Heart's Content.

"In every clime the world around,
  The waste of waters o'er;
An El Dorado have we found,
  That ne'er was found before.
The isles of spice, the lands of dawn,

Where East and West are blent—
All these our eyes have looked upon,
But where is Heart's Content?

"Oh, turn again, while yet ye may,
And ere the hearths are cold,
And all the embers ashen-gray,
By which ye sat of old,
And dumb in death the loving lips
That mourned as forth ye went
To join the fleet of missing ships,
In quest of Heart's Content;

"And seek again the harbor-lights,
Which faithful fingers trim,
Ere yet alike the days and nights
Unto your eyes are dim!
For woe, alas! to those that roam
Till time and tide are spent,
And win no more the port of home—
The only Heart's Content!"

AUTHOR UNKNOWN

LIFE'S LESSONS

I learn, as the years roll onward
    And leave the past behind,
That much I had counted sorrow
    But proves that God is kind;
That many a flower I had longed for
    Had hidden a thorn of pain,
And many a rugged bypath
    Led to fields of ripened grain.

The clouds that cover the sunshine
    They can not banish the sun;
And the earth shines out the brighter
    When the weary rain is done.
We must stand in the deepest shadow
    To see the clearest light;
And often through wrong's own darkness
    Comes the very strength of light.

The sweetest rest is at even,
    After a wearisome day,
When the heavy burden of labor
    Has borne from our hearts away;

And those who have never known sorrow
    Can not know the infinite peace
That falls on the troubled spirit
    When it sees at least release.

We must live through the dreary winter
    If we would value the spring;
And the woods must be cold and silent
    Before the robins sing.
The flowers must be buried in darkness
    Before they can bud and bloom,
And the sweetest, warmest sunshine
    Comes after the storm and gloom.

AUTHOR UNKNOWN

WHEN I HAVE TIME

WHEN I have time so many things I'll do
To make life happier and more fair
For those whose lives are crowded now with care;
I'll help to lift them from their low despair
    When I have time.

When I have time the friend I love so well
Shall know no more these weary, toiling days;
I'll lead her feet in pleasant paths always
And cheer her heart with words of sweetest praise,
    When I have time.

When you have time! The friend you hold so dear
May be beyond the reach of all your sweet intent;
May never know that you so kindly meant
To fill her life with sweet content
    When you had time.

Now is the time! Ah, friend, no longer wait
To scatter loving smiles and words of cheer
To those around whose lives are now so drear;
They may not need you in the coming year—
    Now is the time!

AUTHOR UNKNOWN